# ANOTHER BEAUTIFUL SUNDAY

## KAREN BROWNE

An anthology of poetry

Written during lockdown

2020 - 2021

First paperback edition 2022

Cover design by John Brown


Editors
Liam Dixon, H Rickett-Browne and B Browne

ISBN 9798731244008

Published and printed by
www.kindlepublishingincome.com

# ACKNOWLEDGEMENT

It wasn't until the first Covid-19 lockdown 2020 that I began to write poetry. I have Parkinson's Disease and at that time was considered to be in a vulnerable group, so had to isolate at home for twelve weeks. It was one Sunday afternoon during this time that I sat playing with words. The result is the poem 'Another Beautiful Sunday'. Until then I had never written anything at all. I belong to a lovely Parkinson's support group, and I mentioned to them that I had started to write poetry and was delighted when I was invited to join their poetry group. The support and encouragement I have received from this group has been invaluable. I wish to thank everyone especially Jan Sargent EdD, MA, poet/artist, who has been my mentor and has encouraged me to continue to write, helping me to build up my confidence in my writing. I now consider Jan a dear friend, so thank you Jan for everything.

Many people have asked me why I don't publish my poems into a book. Well, I took up their suggestion and here it is.

I have so many people to thank for their continuing support, including my lovely family, friends and former work colleagues.

I could not have got this far without the help of my son in law Liam. I am hopeless with anything technical and must have driven him to distraction with me constantly asking him how/what/when and where, while going through the process of self-publishing this book.

My two daughters Helen and Beth have the patience of saints. They proofread all of my poems, with me constantly changing my mind as to which ones I wanted to be included.

Thank you too, to John Brown (my dear school friend since we were nine years old) for designing the book cover for me.

My poems have grown from a wide range of subjects and emotions, including the highs and lows of living with Parkinson's Disease, and the fear and frustrations of living through a pandemic.

# Contents

ACKNOWLEDGEMENT .................................................3

WORDS ...............................................................9

ANOTHER BEAUTIFUL SUNDAY ...............................10

IN THE EYES OF A CHILD .......................................12

PEONIES .............................................................13

SILLY O'CLOCK .....................................................14

TODAY IS A GOOD DAY ..........................................15

A LOVE SO TRUE ..................................................17

AS I STAND AT MY WINDOW ...................................19

ANOTHER DAY ......................................................20

VE DAY 8th MAY 2020............................................21

A YEAR HAS PASSED BY .........................................23

I DO NOT UNDERSTAND..........................................25

DO THEY KNOW YOUR NAME ..................................27

NO RUSHING ........................................................29

THE COUNTRY PARK..............................................31

THE LOFT .............................................................33

CAKE ..................................................................35

TURMOIL .............................................................37

PLASTIC RULER .....................................................38

MR PARKY ...........................................................39

TELL YOU WHAT ...................................................41

IT'S SNOWING ......................................................43

THEY ANSWERED THE CALL ....................................45

WHO AM I? ...................................................47

YOU ARE YOU ...............................................48

THE SHED ....................................................49

DATING........................................................50

LITTLE MEEP MEEP........................................51

MASSACRE...................................................52

RAINDROPS ..................................................53

MEMORIES ...................................................54

DISARRAY ....................................................56

FIRST DAY AT SCHOOL....................................57

EXAM DAY ....................................................58

SUNDAY AFTERNOON .....................................59

DREAMS ......................................................60

ENOUGH.......................................................61

TODAY .........................................................62

MY WEARY HEAD ..........................................63

MISSING GLASSES .........................................64

SPOONS.......................................................65

ONE OF THESE DAYS ......................................66

LITTLE BEE ...................................................68

MY LITTLE FRIEND .........................................69

THE PROMISE OF A NEW SPRING.......................70

BAKING DAY .................................................71

DEPRESSION .................................................72

HAVE YOU SEEN THE TIME...............................73

THE WIND....................................................74

ONCE IN A WHILE .......................................75

AS THE INK FLOWS ....................................76

IS IT TOO EARLY?.......................................77

MY WOODEN STABLE ................................78

AT THE TOP OF THE CHRISTMAS TREE .....................79

SNOWMAN..................................................80

CHRISTMAS MORNING...............................81

NO MAN'S LAND .......................................83

NEW YEAR'S EVE .......................................84

JANUARY ....................................................86

A TRUE FRIEND...........................................87

IF.................................................................88

DAY AFTER DAY ..........................................89

THE FIRST STEP ...........................................90

WHEN? ......................................................91

ARE WE NEARLY THERE YET? ......................92

TIRED ..........................................................94

LITTLE IDEA................................................95

THE FAN .....................................................97

WHY ME ...!!! .............................................98

THE TELEPHONE .........................................99

NOT A SINGLE WORD ...............................100

23rd JUNE................................................102

YOU WAIT.................................................104

WHEN YOU FEEL SO LOW .......................................105

LONELINESS...........................................................106

HAVE YOU EVER WONDERED...............................107

MOTHER'S DAY......................................................108

MY DAD .................................................................109

LESLIE MALCOLM ..................................................110

MY OLD FRIEND.....................................................111

THE FINAL COUNTDOWN......................................112

BUTTER ON MY TOAST..........................................113

CLICKETY CLACK ...................................................114

SITTING IN THE VETS.............................................116

SOME DAYS ...........................................................117

WE DO GET THERE ................................................118

WHAT IS POETRY ..................................................120

SO WHAT...............................................................121

## WORDS

To be able to use words
To be able to tell a story
Whether it be happy
Or whether it be sad
To be able to use words
To make yourself hear
To commiserate
Or revel in glory
To watch these words
Perform their magic
Is sure delight
Just beware
Just take care
They are not used to spite
To decry
To put down
For that would be tragic
Use words to tell your story
Whether it be happy
Whether it be sad
But not to hurt or bully
To tarnish or sully
But the spirit to lift
For that in itself
Is surely a gift

## ANOTHER BEAUTIFUL SUNDAY

It is another beautiful Sunday
The sun is shining
The birds are singing
In their gardens the children playing
In the distance church bells are ringing
It is another beautiful Sunday
The gardeners are busy
The flowers begin to bloom
Families are chilling
Dinner is cooking
It is another beautiful Sunday
But all is not as it seems
A dark cloud brings sadness and doom
Horror not imagined in nightmare dreams
Evil has swept the earth
Not caring if young, old, or sick
Some will survive
Death does not come quick
But slow and lonely
No loved one at your side
It is still a beautiful Sunday
People are told stay home, stay safe
Do not socialise or mix
While scientists search for a fix
Thousands have died
Thousands are still dying
You are told to stay inside
To try to stop the spread
Of this evil virus

But this request many of you are defying
So many more will be dead
But it is still a beautiful Sunday

(This is the first poem I had ever written.
It was during the first lockdown of
2020)

## IN THE EYES OF A CHILD

The garden, in the eyes of a child
Can be a magical place
Seeing the awe upon his face
As he watches the ants scurry on their way
Marching two by two
Is priceless
His eyes shine with wonder as the butterfly
Flitters and flutters her dainty wings
As the little Robin joins him on the lawn
Waiting patiently as he searches
For her a wiggly worm
To him she sings
The look on his face is priceless
He giggles as a ladybird gently lands
Upon the flowerpot which contains
The precious apple seeds he has planted,
Waiting in hope
For the "big giant trees' that will grow
In his young mind hopefully by tomorrow
The look on his face is priceless
This magic and wonder cannot be bought
They must be loved and nurtured
And treasured
These times are so very precious
Memories such as these are priceless

## PEONIES

Every year
I watch you begin to appear
From those tiny little shoots
And I watch each day in awe
As your stems grow tall
Secure within your roots
Snug beneath the earth
To start your rebirth
Blooms more and more
Of you appear
Each and every one
Reaching up towards
The warmth of the sun
Gently swaying in the soft
Cool breeze
Ladybirds and butterflies
Visit you along with the busy bees
Your beauty is my pride and joy
Blooms so pretty and pink
A few weeks you stay
So, your beauty I can enjoy
Then with a heavy sigh
The signs begin to show
That for this year you are done
Sadly, it is time for you to go
But I know for sure next year
You will return here
My one and only
My beautiful Peony

## SILLY O'CLOCK

It's half past silly o'clock
In the morning
All I want to do is sleep
I lay here tossing and turning
I have lost count of how many flippin' sheep
Are skipping around the room
All I want to do is sleep
I put on some pretty music
They say it is calming and soothing
But I tell you now if I don't get some sleep
It is my mind I will be losing
I am still awake at silly o'clock
In the early hours of the morning
I lay here trying to relax
And stop the incessant yawning
All I want is some sleep
So off I go to make a warm drink
Making more noise trying to be quiet
As the spoon clatters in the sink
The "not hot" cross buns look oh so very tempting
Ah well tomorrow I'll restart my diet
And back to bed I go
Then ouch I stub my effing toe
I'm still awake at silly o'clock
Please all I want is some sleep
The new day is dawning
And the blessed birds begin to cheep
I cannot believe it is already nearly morning
All I want is some flippin' sleep

## TODAY IS A GOOD DAY

It is in the silence
It is in the darkness
Of the sleepless night
That the mind begins to run
Filled with thoughts
Of the day before
Of the eggshells
Tiptoed on once more
Of the feeling of dread
As the key turns
In the door
The fear deep inside
That begins to churn
Hearing the footsteps
Come ever nearer
As you wonder will today
Be a good day
Where just for a while
You can breathe
You can smile
You look at the face before you
And today is going to be a good day
There are flowers
And a gentle kiss

An endearment of affection
Today is going to be a good day
But that fear that churns deep inside
Will never leave
Because you know in your heart
Tomorrow may not be a good day

(That feeling of dread that many domestic abuse
sufferers go through)

## A LOVE SO TRUE

Ours is a love so true
The minute I saw you
I just knew
You were the one for me
But of our love
We could no one tell
None we wanted to
Hurt or harm
Our meetings kept
Behind closed doors
Where I would just melt
In your arms
We were happy in our
Innocent bliss
Till that fateful day
We were caught red handed
As you stroked my hair
And my head about to kiss
The key turned in the door
But it was too late
I ran leaving you
To face your fate
Over the fence I flew
In the garden I landed
I slinked back home
And as I licked my paws
I hoped in anticipation

The fact I am a cat
Would be enough explanation
And that I am prepared to
Share him with you
His one and only love truly
His exasperated Julie

## AS I STAND AT MY WINDOW

As I stand at my window I smile
For I can see before me
As far as the eye can see
Mile after mile
Of the prettiest scenery
A joy to be seen
Fields laid out in squares
Or shapes of all sizes
Colours of yellow, brown and green
Each holding its own surprises
Within its crops of barley and wheat
This sight I will treasure
For soon it will be no more
The picture of beauty
Sadly, will be gone
For many a year a battle has raged
In the hope that it would be saved
But to no avail
Houses are to sprout on concrete fields
Roads and pavements were
Crops once upon a time would yield
Bringing with it noise and pollution
So I stand and look out my window
And treasure the sight before me
Because it will be gone tomorrow

## ANOTHER DAY

As you by the door stand
Staring at the key
In your sweat covered hand
Not quite able to understand
The fear about to overwhelm you
Not knowing what to do
As you stand there
Staring at the key
In your sweat covered hand
You turn to walk away
As you visibly shake
And off your coat you take
You tell yourself
I can do this another day
As you stare at the key
In your sweat covered hand
Can't I?
Well maybe, just maybe.

(I felt like this one Saturday after an incident at my former
workplace, I found it difficult to leave my house when it came
to my next shift)

## VE DAY 8th MAY 2020

The bunting gently flutters in
The early morning breeze
The windows, with poppies
On proud display
The smell of baking
Wafting from the kitchen
Coffee and scones,
Cake and tea

Made ready for the PM's speech
At half past three,
The grass is mown
The weeds no more
Everything is ready
It is VE Day
75 years celebration
Of the ending of the Wa

But it is a party with a difference
All observing social distance
Remembering those who gave
The ultimate
The Heroes of that generation
And scores more since
At eleven o'clock
On the dot
Two minutes silence
Will be held

They will never be forgot
So much they gave
For our freedom
Today we party
Raise our glasses
And remember them

## A YEAR HAS PASSED BY

A year has passed
Since total lockdown was
Declared
Stay home stay inside
From the enemy unseen
To be known as Covid19
Tears have been cried
Thousands have sadly died
Untold heartbreak and grief
A year has passed by
Life as we knew it is no more
Self-isolating
Social distancing
No more hugging
Those you adore
Sad faces wave from windows
Many adorned with pictures of rainbows
No longer our heroes' athletes
Or celebrities
But Key Workers of every group
So many to mention
Namely our beloved NHS
Mandatory wearing of masks
Praying for the prevention
Of more infection
As we celebrate a new vaccine

A year has gone by
In silence we stand
With candles in our hand
And as we reflect
We must never forget
The loved ones lost
And their loved ones left behind

## I DO NOT UNDERSTAND

I do not understand
Why I cannot hold your hand
It seems so unfair
That I cannot share
A hug or two
Even with you
Mummy says we must
Listen
To the rules of social distance
But I do not understand
Why I cannot hold your hand
Mummy says it is a nasty germ
That wants to cause us harm
I still do not understand
Why I cannot hold your hand
Mummy says if we do cuddle
We might end up in hospital
So, every night I pray
That one wonderful day
This horrible time will end
And we no longer have to spend
Our time listening
To the rule of social distancing
And at last
As we did in the past

I can let you know
How I miss
You so
And give you a big big kiss
A squeezy squeezy hug
And
Mummy will say I can hold your hand.


(One of the heart-breaking aspects of the rules of
Social distancing was not being able hug your
Grandchildren if they did not live in your 'bubble')

## DO THEY KNOW YOUR NAME

Do they know your name?
Do they even care?
Every day is the same
Just as long as you are there
Putting up with attitude
With always a smile
Whether on the till
Or in the aisle
The Bakery
The Butchery
Deli and Fish Bar
Oven Fresh or Cafeteria
The Kiosk
Produce dept
And FFPP
Not forgetting Admin
And Personnel too
Do they know your name?
Do they even care?
No longer is it famous celebrities
That we adore
But Nurses, Doctors, Care Home
Workers, Vets and Cleaners
Teachers, Child Carers galore
Train drivers, Bus drivers
Truck drivers and Bin men too
Postal Workers, Volunteers,
Warehouse Workers,
Delivery drivers too,

Care Workers in the community,
Taxi drivers,
Pharmacies, GP surgeries,
Paramedics
Police and Fire Services,
So many of you all to mention
and to have left out any of you
Is so not my intention
Now do they know your name
Now do they care
As long as you are there
(edited)

## NO RUSHING

It is the silence
The lack of hustle and bustle
No rushing or pushing
No standing around
Enjoying a chit or a chat
Gossiping about this or that
Those you do see
Are in a hurry
Their faces lined with worry
Wearing their mask
As they go about their task
An air of sadness seeps around
The once busy centre of town
Most have been listening
To the rules of social distancing
No more handshakes
No more hugs
Going against human nature
The gradual shutdown
Of the long lockdown
Begins with hopeful belief
The new vaccine will bring relief
And that one day
In the future not too long
The silence will have gone

The hustle and bustle
The rushing or pushing
The standing around
Enjoying a chit and a chat
Gossiping about this or that
And getting in every one's way
Will be back one day

## THE COUNTRY PARK

The sun is shining high above
In the sky so blue
Its warmth caressing
Everything within its touch

The newly grown buds
Upon the many branches
Of tall straight trees

Softly swaying in the gentle breeze
They begin to open
And share their secrets

With leaves of every shade of green
Forming a soft cool canopy
Just a chink of light here and there
Revealing the wonders
Upon the ground
Where many forms of life
Can surely be found
From the smallest of them all
The ants scurrying two by two
In almost military formation
As busy as the buzzing bees
Flying from flower to flower
Creating pollination
Encouraging each bloom to share
Their pretty heads of colour
Butterflies flitter and flutter
Their dainty wings
Little ladybirds with coats so red
And shiny black spots

The tiny dormouse fast asleep
Tucked away in his little nest
Bluebells and buttercups
And daisies too
Dandelions with their heads
Of fluffy white clocks
Loved by every generation
Birds singing their song
Insects and bugs, rabbits and deer
Foxes and badgers
So many more to mention
Do not be fooled by the illusion
Of silence
Stop just for a moment or two
And listen to and watch the wonders
 Of the world around you
As the sun smiles from the sky
So high above
Spreading her warmth and love
Throughout the precious legacy
Of your local country park

## THE LOFT

A room full of
Boxes and bags
The contents long forgotten
Stored for that rainy day
Or just in case
You just never know
The dog-eared treasured books
From a childhood long ago
Stories that took your
Imagination
On many an adventure
The tattered teddy
Once very much loved
Who never left your side
Now stored away
Almost totally forgotten
Until today
A wash and a brush up
Now on your bed he will stay
Boxes of photos galore
Of loved ones long gone
Memories return
Of the happy times
Of sad times too
A battered old suitcase
Seen better days
Christmas tree baubles
And streams of tinsel too
Lie within this suitcase

Waiting patiently for the tree
To adorn once more
You look around you
And with a smile
You decide
These boxes and bags
Full of trinkets and treasures
With memories too precious to discard
Can stay
At least until that rainy day

## CAKE

Sponge Cake
Fruit Cake
Lemon drizzle ...
Simnel cake
(Marzipan! ... oh yay)
Christmas cake, birthday cake
My goodness
I will be here all day
So many to chose
Cakes galore
But the one
Always a choice of mine
So yummy, so divine
Must be the ultimate
It must be chocolate
After the morning
I have had
For a slice I shall be so glad
Cascades of water did pour
On opening the washer's door
For sanity's sake
I need cake
But I cry in despair
Searching high and low
Oh, woe is me, oh woe
There is no cake
No cake .... anywhere
Can no one else see my desperation
Does no one care
As I implore you
To take pity

There is no cake anywhere
Flour, eggs, sugar,
Cocoa powder and butter
Ready and waiting in the bowl
To be beaten and whisked
My solution to be fixed
Soon there will be cake
And I will be in heaven
For a short while at least
As I see the wonderful creation
My salvation
A chocolate cake
In all its glory
My sanity restored

## TURMOIL

The early hours of the morning
So quiet, so peaceful,
Not a sound can be heard
No traffic in the distance
Not even the song of a bird
But it is this time of hour that I find
Thoughts and memories
Dreams and nightmares
Invade my mind
A tightly wound cog,
Churning and spinning
Like some wild maelstrom
With the world around me
In complete turmoil
Sleep evades me
No relief from the fog
Which lays like a heavy blanket
On my mind

## PLASTIC RULER

When I see you, I think of my dad
Many years now he has been gone
When I see you, I don't feel sad
You are from a time now long gone
My affection for you may seem peculiar
And you I certainly do treasure
After all you are just a plastic ruler
Not by metric do you measure
But by inches imperial
It is a rule unspoken
That no one dare you touch
Heaven forbid if you were broken
It would hurt me so much
With much care you are put away
Until I need your help another day

(The result of using any object as subject of a
creative writing exercise)

## MR PARKY

Go away
I don't want you here
I didn't invite you
Into my life
Go away
How much more
Do I need
To say to you
To make it clear
Enough is enough
It isn't too much to ask
For you to give me a break
Life's simple pleasures
From me you take
So much I can do no more
From brushing my hair
To cleaning my teeth
Slowly you try to steal my dignity
Leaving me with tremors
And rigidity
But I want you to know
You will not win
With me you have a fight
I will not give in
So Mr Parky

If you don't mind
Would you be so kind
To shut the door behind
You as you go
And just so you know
You are not going to win
I am dammed if I will give in

(Parkinson's is a cruel disease and no two days are
ever the same.)

## TELL YOU WHAT

Tell you what ... step in my shoes
Go on just for one day
See if you can cope
It isn't a game
You don't win, you hopefully
Do not lose
But maybe, I can always hope
Your attitude, your opinion
Will no longer be the same
And you will learn, you will see
Just what day to day
Life is like for me
It's the little things
That come to mind
That you will find
Not as easy to do
As you used to be able to
Brushing your hair
Pulling up your drawers
Doing up buttons
Pulling up zips
Puling the strangest of faces
While doing up your boot laces
Walk with a stick because your
Balance has gone
That is just a teeny example

Of my life day after day
The list is so long
If you have a problem with me
Just come to my face and say
Tell you what ... I will step in your shoes
Just for a day

(Written after a unwarranted comment about my
Parkinson's)

## IT'S SNOWING

It's snowing, it's snowing
Came the excited cry
Just what is it about snow
That has both adult and child
Running to the window
To watch the snow fall
Hoping upon hope it will settle
Upon the ground
It's snowing, it's snowing
Again came the cry
Can we play out
Came the excited shout
Come on mum, come on dad
There are snowball fights to be had
And snowmen to build
Everyone is wrapped up warm
Against the cold
The fun starts in earnest
For both young and old
The snowballs begin to fly around you
There is only one thing for you to do
And that is to join in the fun
With everyone
Many a sledge
Are pulled from garage or shed
Snowmen are
Dressed in dad's old clothes
A bobble hat, scarf and gloves
And a borrowed carrot for his nose

The hours soon fly by
Now it is time to go home
News greeted with moans
There is always tomorrow
The adults they say
With a smile
Because today
Just for a little while
They could pretend Covid had gone away

## THEY ANSWERED THE CALL

They answered the call
They joined the fight
For the male dominated right
to vote ... for all
Brave souls they were too
What they went through
Just for a taste of equality
But they were seen as a threat
Expected to stay at home
Tied to the kitchen sink
Banned from thoughts of their own
God forbid if they for themselves dared to think
These delicate stupid females
In the male-controlled opinion
Enough was enough
The fight ahead would be tough
But many answered the call
To join the fight
For the right
To vote ... for all
Tying themselves to railings
Marching through the streets
Recruiting as they went
The male population in panic
Seeing themselves as failing
To keep their women folk under control
Prison stays did not deter
These women young and old
Their bravery tested by man's brutality

With the forced feeding
Horror of horrors to unfold
To try to prevent self-starvation
Then came the war of all wars
All the menfolk sent off to fight
To protect their precious nation
Leaving the country needing
The women to take over work
Never before done by the female persuasion
And they came and answered the call
But their fight was not forgotten
And to many to their delight
The right to vote was awarded
It is so important now
To remember just how
Hard fought was the fight
For us women to have the right
To vote ...

## WHO AM I?

Who am I?
I am not going to lie
I am who you see
I am me
No airs and no graces
No two faces
Treat me right
And you will find
With me a friend for life
Someone to care
Someone to share
Good times and bad
Happy and sad
Who am I?
I'm not going to lie
I am who you see
I am me

## YOU ARE YOU

Some days you open your eyes
And raise your weary head
The last thing you want to do is crawl
Out of your beloved bed
But that is perfectly ok
Because the very next day
You could be raring to go
Ready to move mountains
But as you already know
No two days are ever the same
But that is ok too
Because inside you are still you
You are still the person people know and love
We are all each dealt life's card
For some it can be extra hard
So be proud of yourself
And when you do feel sad
Just stop for a little while
And look around you
Focus on what makes you smile
And remind yourself you are doing great

## THE SHED

Whatever possessed me
What was I thinking of
It really did seem like a good idea … at the time
To delve deep into the bowels of the shed
Not knowing what horrors I would find
Amongst the sight of total chaos
As I tentatively tiptoed between
The bags and boxes
Dodging curtains of cobwebs
Searching for the light switch
When suddenly the urge to scream
Overwhelmed me
There perched on the corner
Of the box nearest my head
Watching me closely with his beady eyes
Was the biggest SPIDER I have ever seen
Now I will not have it said
That I am easy to scare
But as for spiders I have no care
So not waiting a second more
I head directly for the open door
Turning the key in the lock
I hear a voice behind me ask
So are we sorting out the shed
Suffice to say I cannot repeat
Without offence my reply

## DATING

Do I? ... don't I?
Oh my oh my
A big decision to be made
One you have been contemplating for a while
On goes your profile
The monthly subscription fees
Almost paid
Do I? don't I?
Oh my oh my
That big decision you have made
After checking and double checking every detail
With a deep breath you send the email
And now you wait ...

## LITTLE MEEP MEEP

The first time I set eyes on you
Dressed in ribbons and balloons
You looked like the belle of the ball
But I just couldn't take to you at all
To me it was a sign of defeat
In my efforts to beat
Mr Parkinson's
It was such a shame
You are so sweet
We have even given you a name
Little Meep Meep
Yet you would patiently sit there
Waiting in vain for me to care
A resting place for the family cat
And you were content with that
Then one day
I came along to say
Little Meep Meep it is your lucky day
We are going for a little tour
Of our local park
So off we 'zoom' thru the side door
Lol such speed, such power
At only four miles an hour
We got there in the end
Didn't we Meep Meep
My little friend
And of adventures galore
I know there will be more

## MASSACRE

To watch I cannot bare
The total massacre
Of what I hold so dear
I am told its for your own good
This absolute desecration
Of flower, fern and wood
(Dead wood apparently)
Give a trim he said
Only for him to find
Your inner branches very dead
No longer a hiding space
So many of you now cut down
And as i look around
In almost despair
I found it unbelievable
That you will still return to me
In full flower and glory
Year after year

## RAINDROPS

What is it about raindrops on the windowpane?
What is the fascination that holds?
Us time and time again
As we sit here watching you
Imagining you both in a race
Always travelling two by two
Moving carefully and slowly
Then picking up your pace
Each of us hoping our chosen
One is the winner
The shouts of victory
When your journey ends
Then the magic is broken
When mum calls us for dinner
So off we go on our way
Promising to meet you again
On another rainy day

# MEMORIES

As I lay here wide awake
Yet again
My mind runs away
With memories,
Some good, some bad
Many happy, many sad
Of the years gone by
And of those I have loved
And lost on the way
It would be so easy to recall
A magical childhood
Seen through rose tinted glasses
Protected from heartache and heartbreak
By the best parents of all
Living in a small village
Everyone knowing Everyone
Safe in the knowledge
I could knock on any door
As a young child
I could wish for no more
Long summer holidays
Spent in play
Bucket in hand off to the
Brook we would go
Catching crayfish,
Sticklebacks and the odd one or two
Unsuspecting minnow
Vowing to nurture and protect them
As onwards back home

I would return
My exasperated mum
Would shake her head
Allowing them in the house was a big no
So, on the doorstep instead
There they are left
But when I return, I am completely bereft
My beloved catch is all
Laying on their sides ...
Very dead
A hard life's lesson to learn
I did what I had to do
On mum's orders flushed
Them down the loo
My sorrow soon forgotten
As I begin another adventure
Of picnics by the canal
Weekly visits to church and chapel
So many wonderful memories to mention
This childhood bliss
Soon came to an end
When we moved to town life
I was nine years old
And another chapter of my life begins
Ready to be told

## DISARRAY

I sit here and look around me
The room is in complete disarray
Around the living room floor
The little train track winds its way
Engines and carriages discarded
Trucks and cars galore
These toys bestowed with so much love
By a little boy now tucked up in bed
Fast asleep, in his room above
In his three-year-old innocence
Totally unaware
That the room below
Is in complete disarray
And as I look around me
I find I really do not care
A home full of toys
In my eyes
Is a home full of love

## FIRST DAY AT SCHOOL

As you stand at the school gate
With a tear or two in your eye
Waiting for your little one to turn around and wave
goodbye
You wonder where already that has time gone
Since the day he was born
A tiny mite helpless in your arms
With whom you fell hopelessly in love
Promising to cherish and keep from life's harm
Watching and nurturing
Treasuring each milestone
At last, reaching this day
Your heart filled with trepidation
His with unconcealed excitement
It is the very first day at school
And as you watch and wait with a tear or two in
your eye
He turns round and with the biggest smile
And he waves goodbye
Not a tear on his face in sight
You know then by him you have done right

## EXAM DAY

The day is here
The day has arrived
And you feel sick with fear
All those hours you
Have studied and revised
You pray will be enough
You sit there
At the blank page and you stare
Your mouth feels dry
You feel like you could cry
You look at the door
Through it you want to run
Until you can run no more
Then it is starting orders
And off you go ... not ...
Till you tell yourself
This is one chance you have got
To do your very best
And to have faith in yourself
When the clock stops the time
The relief you feel for now
Is that it is over
That is it until the results
And that is not till October

## SUNDAY AFTERNOON

It is Sunday afternoon
Everyone is gathered in the room
A game of chess is being played
Kinetic sandcastles being made
The roast cooking merrily away
A lovely way to spend a Sunday
Mums having a good old chat
About this and about that
Grandma sitting in the corner
Having a quick nap
The family cat curled upon her lap
Dads in full discussion having a lot to say
A lovely way to spend a Sunday
Dinner has been served
Not a sound can be heard
Apart from the tippety tap of knives and forks
All too busy eating to talk
A lovely way to spend a Sunday
These moments you cannot measure
But are moments to treasure

## DREAMS

We all have our dreams
For some they come true
For some it always seems
No matter what they do
These dreams are just out of reach
But maybe they are not the ones for you
Maybe you are reaching a tad too high
But then who am I
To dare suggest
That your dreams
Are not as worthy as the rest
Your dreams belong to you
And maybe just maybe they will come true
We all dream of a life filled with happiness
With people we love and adore
For some this is never enough
And strive for much more
We really do have to take heed
Of what dreams to come true we really need
For me it isn't immense wealth
It is a happy family and good health
One out of two isn't so bad
Nothing I can do so it is pointless being sad
I can still have my dreams
Because they belong to me

## ENOUGH

When you think you have had enough
When you know you already have your fair share
And life for you often feels tough
One more thing is thrown at you
One more thing to have to grin and bare
You begin to think why?
And that it just isn't fair
But all the time you try to carry on
Not telling others that something is wrong
Giving the impression that you are very strong
As you greet them with yet another smile
They do not see the tears you cry
When it gets too much
These tears no one else will get to see
You alone will feel sorry for you
Then you will do what you always do
Get up and brush yourself down
Walk out that door with a smile
(Not a frown)
And get on with your day

## TODAY

Today is not a good day
Joints and muscle stiff with pains
Yesterday was a good day
I could have moved mountains
Today is not a good day
Today I hate my Parkinson's
Tomorrow is a mystery
I have no idea what it will bring
Today is a bad day
I can barely function
After a long night that would keep
Me deprived of much needed sleep
Today is a bad day
I could for myself feel sorrow
But what is the point
Parkinson's is here with me to stay
Today is a bad day
But maybe just maybe a good day
It will be tomorrow

## MY WEARY HEAD

Do you ever sit there or stand
And your mind goes blank
Not really registering
What is going on around you
Daydreaming they call it
Frustrating more like
I know I have something to do
So why did I come upstairs
Ah well I might as well go
For a tiddle while I am up here
Then why did I come into the room
I stand there for a while
Trying to recollect
Amongst the muddle in my head
Then I begin to smile
As I spy my beloved bed
Relieved after all to find
That I am not actually losing my mind
I am just exhausted from a long day at work
For I am never one to shirk
Times are tough for everyone
No one knows when it will end
But for this moment now
I lay my weary head
And to everyone for tomorrow
I wish you a good day
But for now, all I wish to say
Is goodnight
And sleep tight.

## MISSING GLASSES

Ok so I make an appointment
With the opticians
Covid19 rules to apply
Of course
Bring your glasses they say
Which I would do anyway
These glasses I wear day after day
So of course
They just have to disappear
Off the face off the earth
I have searched here
And I have searched there
I have searched everywhere
And no, they are not on my head
Now I am in despair
So off I go
And when I get there
I was told "oh that's ok,
You didn't need to bring them anyway

## SPOONS

Spoons
Every day
Mundane objects
Taken for granted
Big spoons
Little spoons
Dessert spoons
Tablespoons
All sizes galore
Not forgetting
Our beloved teaspoons
All snug and cosy in the
Cutlery drawer
But wait what us this
The little teaspoons are
Becoming no more
One by one off they go
To where nobody knows
Where they have gone
I am in despair
(Does anyone really care)
Please can someone help me
Solve one of life's
Greatest mysteries

## ONE OF THESE DAYS

I smile as I watch you try
So hard to catch that bird
The way It sits there
And taunts you are quite absurd
It waits as you run around
And around the garden
Waiting for it to land
Upon the ground
You crouch and you creep
Almost like the cat
Who incidentally is fast asleep
Under the rose bush
Bored with your antics
You are so still,
Not a muscle does flinch
The bird it watches you
From the corner of its eye
When suddenly it takes flight
Across the garden
Just out of your reach
In your surprise
And in your rush
You are the funniest of sights
As you yap
In sheer frustration
The bird it sits on the shed
Watching you with a tilt
Of its head
Yet again it has the last laugh

As you trot back up the path
Another major fail
You look back at the bird
With a wag of your tail
As if to say
Watch out little bird
Tomorrow is another day

## LITTLE BEE

Watching you with fascination
As you go on your way
Mesmerized as you fly
From flower to flower
This you do every day
It is still early morning
The new day has done with dawning
It is well and truly here
The sky cloudless and blue
But as I watch you do you care
Are you even aware
Of the beauty around you
As you busy yourself flying
 From here to there
Stopping on occasion
To spread your tiny wings
Almost as if you are listening
To the birds in full song
Spying the spider watching you
Her web covered in silver dew
Glistening in the early morning sun
Then back home you go
To your little wooden house
Tiny bamboo poles lined in a row
And how I wish I could spy
On you as you disappear inside
Each little doorway sealed with a leaf
The magic and wonder
Almost beyond belief
I wish you good day
As I go on my own way

## MY LITTLE FRIEND

Hello my little friend
It is so lovely to see you again
As the new day is dawning
And the world begins to awake
Fluffy white clouds sail like ships above
In the sky so blue
The sun is smiling
It is going to be a lovely day
The birds with all their heart
Begin to sing
So much joy does their music bring
And you my little friend
What has your song have to say
As you patiently watch
And patiently wait
To see what treat I have for you today
As I hold out my hand
With complete trust in me
And a flutter of your dainty little wings
With a hop and a skip, you land
So little and light
So sweet, eyes alert and bright
You take what I offer
Then away you go
My little Robin Redbreast
Same place same time tomorrow
Till then stay safe my little friend

## THE PROMISE OF A NEW SPRING

Tomorrow can bring
Many a wonder
Like the promise of the new Spring
The rebirth of the leaves on the trees
Little green shoots emerging
From their winter sanctuary
Searching for warmth of the sun
The local wildlife taking tentative steps
To abandon hibernation
For this year at least
Birds busy rebuilding nests
For their precious eggs
Lambs in the fields
Jumping and skipping on disorientated legs
The beauty of the little spring flowers
As they emerge shyly from the ground
So, as you worry and you wonder
What will tomorrow bring
Just stop for a moment or two
And about you look around
And you will see
Before you the magic of
What tomorrow can bring

## BAKING DAY

Waking up on a Saturday morning as a child
Was always such a treat
Mum had already been busy baking
The most wonderful goodies to eat
Cakes and biscuits, pies galore
Flapjacks that would guarantee to draw
Mum's best friend carrying a tin
Which would be filled to the brim
They would sit at the table having a good old natter
And maybe a cup of tea or two
Waiting for whatever was in the oven to bake
Mum and her friend would chatter some more
The house filled with wonderful aroma
As mum opened the oven door
Her friend off home she would go
In her hand a carrier bag she would take
Inside her tin filled to the brim
And a chocolate sponge cake
Those days have now long gone
But the memory will always stay
Of wonderful Saturday mornings ...
Mum's baking day

## DEPRESSION

It hits you when you least expect
No rhyme, no reason, no respect
One moment you may be feeling fine
Then next no longer for you does the sun shine
A blackness works into your soul
That feeling of hopelessness and despair
Plunging you into a deep dark hole
Coming from you know not where
In your mind you scream and you shout
But no one hears
Desperately you fight for your way out
No one notices your tears
All this time, all this while
You hide your terror with your smile
They say you are so strong
But just how much more can you take
Of what life throws at you
Before you break
And still, you try as you might
To climb out of that hole
Away from the evil of depression
Which tries to claim your soul
It is a fight you do not choose
You have so much more of life to give
This battle you cannot lose
While you have so much life to live

## HAVE YOU SEEN THE TIME

Really Beau ... have you not seen the time
Do you really need to go out
Have you not seen the time
Oh well on the lead you go
Because madam all your tricks
I have got to know
Into the deep dark depths
Of the garden you will run
Yapping as you go
Waking up everyone
So patiently I stand there
Waiting for you to do
What you need to do
Into the darkness I stare
My imagination running away from me
Wondering what is lurking out there
You stop in your tracks
Ears on alert listening to every sound
Thats enough for me
Back we go inside
Me sighing with relief
As behind us I lock the door
Leaving outside our imagination
And back to bed we go once more
And even though it half past three
In the morning
And the stirrings of a new day are dawning
Despite the pain that you are Beau
I really do love you sooo

## THE WIND

You begin your journey
Steady and slow
Building up your strength as you grow
In the darkness of the night
Becoming as loud as you might
Sweeping through the gardens
Then teasing as you tip toe,
Creeping and prowling
Lulling a sense of serenity
This is a game you like to play
As you look for your next victim
Usually, the solitary rubbish bin
Spewing its contents held within
Or the garden chair
Swept up in your embrace
Flying through the air
It then begins,
The dreaded sound
The incessant howling
That can instil fear
In anyone still around
Sending shivers down the spine
The banging and clattering
Following your path of chaos
As the morning begins to dawn
The evidence of your visit
Is scattered all over the lawn
And the silence returns
Until next time

## ONCE IN A WHILE

Sometimes it is good to stop
Just once in a while
And look around you
And see the things that make
You smile
From the people in your life
That fill your heart with joy
And love
To the sunset and sunrise
And the stars up above
The friendships that have stood
The test of time
It is good to stop
Once in a while
And be thankful for the good things
That make you smile
Even when times are tough
And you wonder why
Bad things are sent your way
Your patience to try
And you feel you have had enough
Just stop for a little while
Focus on the good things
That make you smile.

## AS THE INK FLOWS

Words can easily flow
Leaving their magical
Trail behind them
Weaving into your imagination
Spinning tale after tale
To be able to write
And watch in awe
As the ink flows
And see these words appear
Before you
Is a wonder beyond delight
Then Mr P decides he is here to stay
And you watch with sadness
Your ability to write
Gradually fade away
But no two days are ever the same
Today you may write a novel
Tomorrow maybe not even your name
But do not despair
Although it is not the same
You can still watch with awe and wonder
With the technology out there

## IS IT TOO EARLY?

Is it too early I hear some cry
For what? I ask them why
To put up the Christmas tree of course
But it is only November
Can you not wait until December
No of course not is the retort
I secretly smile
Because with them I agree
Just for this year
Will be the early appearance of my own Christmas
tree
To bring a little joy and cheer
For what has been for many a rotten year
With the treasured decorations
And the untangling of the tree lights
Always fills my heart with delight
When I see the smiles on my grandchildren's faces
When they come visiting me
And spy my beautiful Christmas tree
Standing so tall and proud
Hoping one of the chocolates
Hanging they will be allowed
But as much as I love my tree
By Boxing Day, I wish from it
The living room to be free
Packed away safe and sound
Back up in the loft
Until next Christmas comes around

## MY WOODEN STABLE

Each year you take pride of place
Once pristine and smart
But now well-worn and falling apart
But you are so very much treasured
The love for you cannot be measured
Each year you take the pride of place
And within your welcoming walls you hold
Characters of the loveliest story ever to be told
Of the precious baby born
On what was to become Christmas morn
Soon the time comes
For you to go back
To the box filled with bubble wrap
Packed away with gentle care
Until it's time for you to come
Back with us and your presence share
Taking up the pride of place
My beloved wooden stable

## AT THE TOP OF THE CHRISTMAS TREE

I sit here serenely at the top of the Christmas tree
Watching the world around me go by
So grateful at last to be out of the dark
To be able to share the Christmas cheer
Albeit sitting up here
On this blessed Christmas tree
Longing to jump down and join the frivolity
My crown somewhat now faded
The rest of me looking rather jaded
Not prepared to be usurped by anyone
A bright shining star one year took my place
To mysteriously appear
One morning in pieces on the floor
No one noticed the naughty grin on my face
Relieved the star was no more
So back there was I
Sat way up high
At the top of the Christmas tree
Watching the world go by
But soon comes the time
And packed away again am I
Safe and secure
Knowing for sure
I will be back next year
Sitting at the top of the Christmas tree

## SNOWMAN

Pretty little snowflakes
How delicate they are
Gently slowly fluttering down
Softly falling to the ground
Covering all in their beautiful
blanket of snow
Children's little faces pressed against the window
Watching in awe
Hoping they will settle
Welly boots on
Warm coats, bobble hats
Scarves and mittens too
Excited giggles can be heard
As they begin in earnest
Building their very own snowman
With button eyes and a carrot nose
They look at him with pride
Before going back inside
But the very next day they find him gone
There is no snowman anymore
Just two button eyes and a carrot nose
Laying on the floor
Where he has gone nobody knows

## CHRISTMAS MORNING

Christmas time as a child was magical
We would wake up one morning
To a Christmas tree standing tall and proud
Adorned with baubles and twinkling lights
Our little faces showing sheer delight
Paper lanterns hanging from the ceiling
Giving our home a real Christmas feeling
The Advent Calendar had started days ago
Counting down the days
With us longing to know
what was behind the door
Of number twenty four
Off to bed we would go on Christmas eve
Listening to the lovely story
Of a baby born
On what became Christmas morn
It doesn't matter whether or not you believe
It is a lovely story to share
And soon we were fast asleep
Despite saying awake we would keep
Then on waking at the end of the bed we would
find
A pillowcase each that Santa had left behind
full of presents for us to enjoy
Excited squeals could be heard by mum and dad
There would be a book, a jigsaw and plasticine
And for me the prettiest dolly I had ever seen

Colouring books and crayons
Chocolate coins and a tangerine
It didn't matter to us that it was only half five in the morning
Mum and Dad bleary eyed and yawning
Trying very hard to share the joy
Of a very excited little girl and little boy.

## NO MAN'S LAND

Well, that is the festive cheer
Almost over for another year
Some Christmas trees are already packed away
Some are waiting until New Year's Day
Several take a visit to the tip
With bags of wrapping paper
Enough to fill a skip
Boxing day dinner just cannot be beaten
Cold meats and bubble and squeak eaten.
Children play
With gifts received on Christmas day
Yet the time between
Now and New Year's Eve
Feels like no man's land
Why it is I don't understand
That we lose track of these days
Especially when back to work we return
Bills still need to be paid
Wages still to earn
Then before you realise it is New Year's Eve
Counting in the New Year
Which you pray, hope, and need to believe
Will be a better one
Than the old year just gone

## NEW YEAR'S EVE
## DECEMBER 31st 2020

New Year's Eve is upon us
Filling us with trepidation
Wondering what the New Year for us has in store
Hoping and praying it's an improvement of the year
gone before
For which many was filled with sadness and
heartbreak
Thanks to an enemy unseen
A nasty little virus known as Covid19
Causing untold worldwide disruption
And well-founded fear
2020 will always be known
As the year
of national lockdown
Of wash your hands, cover your face
Give each other space
Do as the powers to be ask
Wear your mask
But sadly, many are not listening
To the advice of social distancing
Putting everyone at serious risk
But there is a glimmer of light
At the end of the tunnel
Vaccines to help given first to the elderly and the
vulnerable
Key workers rightly so at the top of the list

For they in whatever guise have kept the country
on the go
Everyone a true hero
So when we greet in the New Year
With hope in our hearts
Let us raise a glass or two and give our key workers
an extra cheer

## JANUARY

January is a dreary month
The joy and magic of Christmas gone
Back to reality for everyone
Holiday and weight loss adverts appear
New resolutions made in earnest
Forgotten by the second week at least
And so far away
Does it seem is next payday
Having to survive
On the six-month food supply
Bought before Christmas as a panic buy
Because the store had dared to close for a day
So as January draws to close
What will February bring
Well, nobody knows

## A TRUE FRIEND

A true friend
Is a confidante
A shoulder to cry on
An ear to bend
To keep secrets
Never to be told
A true friend
Will egg you on
Sharing the mischief
Sharing the blame
A true friend is
Always in your heart
As the years pass by
Even when apart
A true friend
Is always there
Words may not
Have been spoken
For a while
A true friend
Will just smile
That bond cannot
Be broken
And as the years go by
As you grow old
You treasure
That friend
With love
In your heart

**IF**

IF is a big word
Where do I start
IF can mean anything
IF this and IF that
IF only I did this
IF only I did that
IF only I had followed my heart
IF only I didn't feel sorry for myself
IF only I didn't feel the need to be heard
IF only I didn't need to explain myself
IF only I could sleep
IF is a waste of emotion
IF only people would understand
IF is a big word
IF you allow it to be
I could go on and on

## DAY AFTER DAY

We come in to work after day
Working our socks off for our monthly pay
Getting to know our customers often by name
Sharing stories of our families and our lives
But sadly, not all are the same
Some believe that they have the god given right
To talk to us retail staff as if we were shite
Especially now the covid19 virus
Seems to be here to stay amongst us
Many certainly not listening
To the rules of social distancing
Some insisting on panic buying
Others while queuing moaning, tutting, and sighing
Yet all the while
We continue to greet them with a hello and a smile
We appreciate and understand the present
situation
Is fraught with worry and tension
But all we ask of you is a little more patience
Ok so we don't always get everything right
We honestly do our very best with all our might
And we still come in to work day after day
Working our socks off for our monthly pay

## THE FIRST STEP

Daughter, sister, mother and ex-wife
You stand at the crossroads of your life
Important choices to be made
Deep in your heart you know
Which path you must follow
You have played your part
In life's plan
As the old door closes
The new one opens
A new chapter starts
That first step is tough
But you have done your share
You have done enough
Now it's time to discover new
Adventures out there


(Written just before I left work for good)

## WHEN?

When you bring your child into the world
You look into his eyes and promise the earth
To love and nurture
To protect and cherish
And do for him your very best
A childhood of which so many can only dream
Until the day he leaves the nest
When does it go so wrong
And the heartache begins
You look back over time
Again and again
Can see no reason or rhyme
You dry your tears and hide the pain
And hope and pray ... maybe one day ...

## ARE WE NEARLY THERE YET?

Are we nearly there yet
Is the excited cry
Are we there yet
If not why
We have been in this car for ever
Are we there yet
Will we ever arrive
It seems we will never
Get to our destination.
Every game has been played
I spy can spy no more
Counted cars, lorries, and bikes galore
Are we ever going to reach
The ever so near, but ever so far away beach
Are we there yet
For the umpteenth time
Mum and dad grimace
Can you see the sea yet
The winner buys the ice cream
Look we have at last arrived
Buckets and spades in hand
We run and head for the sand
Build castles with moats
Dad looks on with pride
At his handiwork
Fish and chips on the promenade
Ice creams and the inevitable donkey ride

Then homeward bound at the end of The day
Wishing we could stay
But tired little sleepy heads are
Ready to be tucked up in their beds
Are we there yet?

## TIRED

Tired is my mind
Tired is my body
Tired of trying so hard
Tired of smiling
When everything hurts
Trying not to whinge or complain
About the constant pain
Tired of yet another
Sleepless night
Tired of the constant fight
Just to get thru the day
Tired of pretending that yes I am ok
Tired of being tired
But this fight he will not yet win
To Parkinson's I say
I am not ready to give in

## LITTLE IDEA

A tiny little idea begins
Way back in your mind
And as it grows
You know it is time
For pen and paper
To start their magic
For the idea to appear
Before your very eyes
But no one else would have a clue
What the imagery means to you
Your scribbles the legacy
Of cruel Mr Parky
To him you say
Each and every day
You are not going to win
I am not ready to give in
There you stand
Materials of your art in your hand
Time flies by
An odd tear of frustration
You may cry
A tweak here and a tweak there
As you strive for perfection
At last, a step back you can take
And smile at the creation before you
The latest celebration cake

Knowing that for a little while just yet
Mr Parky hasn't from you
This joy been able to take.
And now you patiently wait
For the cake's collection
But no comment on the state
of the kitchen will be made
By anyone.


(I love making and decorating cakes,
and am dreading the day Parkinson's
takes that ability away from me)

## THE FAN

The night is quiet
The only sound
To be heard
Is the gentle swish
Of the fan
As its propeller
Whizzes around
Cooling the air
That when passing you by
Feels like a soft downy feather
Caressing your skin
While you toss and you turn
Desperately seeking sleep
The night is quiet
Not a sound can be heard
As it waits patiently
For a sign of the new dawn

## WHY ME ...!!!

Sometimes I just want
To scream and shout
Why me!!!
But what is the point
Nothing will change
The pains in every joint
Are there to stay.
Don't even mention
Parkinsons
He will never
Go away
But surely it is my right
As much as anyone else
To be able to sleep
And not just for an hour
Or two
But the whole night through

## THE TELEPHONE

You sit there quietly in the corner
Minding your own business
Forgotten by everyone
But you don't seem to care
As time ticks along
You do not age
Once in a while you will sing
Your own little song
Once upon a time
You were all the rage
Hands free they did call you
No longer tethered
To a wiry line
Or attached to the wall
Now and then
You would sing your song
And they would answer the call
What secrets have you heard
What stories could you tell
Now you sit quietly
In the corner on the windowsill
You don't seem to mind
Gathering dust as you watch
The world passing you by

## NOT A SINGLE WORD

Not a single one
Not a single word
Come to mind
So where do I start
Where do I find
My precious words
Now long gone
My mind reaches out
Where have they gone
I put pen to paper
Try the keyboard
All to no avail
Then the tears begin to flow
Where did those words go
Words that would invade
My thoughts
That would become my friends
Words which down I would write
Words that come to me in my sleep
Words that would make you laugh
Words that would make you weep
I close my eyes in despair
And way behold
My words they are still there
My mind had been fighting pain

But they are back again
All in a jumble
All in chaos
But do I care
As long as they are there

## 23rd JUNE

When as a bride I walked down
The aisle
I was not aware of the evil
Behind your smile
What I took as your love
Did not prepare me
For the heartache to come
The abuse mentally and
Emotionally
That you inflicted on me and my son
You were very sneaky,
Very Clever
In your mind always right,
Wrong you were never
Bad times became many
Good times were few
Ground down so low,
Terrified of you
When people ask me why did I stay
This is what I always have to say
I was told time and time again
It was a domestic issue
That stays behind closed doors
No one wanted to know
To make it work so hard did I try
But to no avail
Then the bruises they began
You needed no excuse
I knew we had to go

But where I just did not know
But then that awful day came
That I knew away we had to run
After more abuse you inflicted on my son
Enough was enough,
There could be no more
Case packed the night before
It was time at last to go
To catch the train
To sanctuary
To never to return
All those years ago
The best decision I ever made
Knowing we would be safe
23<sup>rd</sup> June
A date I treasure
My decree absolute.

(Edited)

## YOU WAIT

You sit and you wait
The call time clearly shown
But it is late
So you sit and you wait
Not daring to go
Because you just know
That is when the phone will ring
So you sit and you wait
Wondering how much longer it will be
You have somewhere else you need to be
You can wait no more
You ring them back
Only to be told
After being left on hold
"I am sorry my dear, the call is tomorrow, not today "

## WHEN YOU FEEL SO LOW

When you feel so low
When you feel you have no choice
When you think no one can hear your voice
Please listen to me
Look around you and you will see
There are many out there
Who really do care
Who do not wish to grieve
For you if you choose to leave
Maybe this moment you are feeling sad
But you have so much to make you glad
So just reach out
And with your voice shout
Someone will be there
To show that they really do care

## LONELINESS

Loneliness can slowly creep upon you
Of it at first you may not be aware
It is often the little things
That take you by surprise
When you begin to realise
For you there is no one to share
These precious moments
Leaving you sadly longing
To feel the sense of belonging
No one sees your tears
Behind closed doors
No one feels your fear
Of forever being alone
But this loneliness inside you, you keep
Not allowing others to see you weep
As you watch life go by
Wanting to loudly shout
I do not want to be the odd one out
Anymore
So you hope and you pray
That special one will come your way
And to loneliness at last you
You can say goodbye

## HAVE YOU EVER WONDERED

Have you ever wondered how written word began
How the magic of speech itself began
Who decided on the first word
Ever to be written
Who decided on the first word
Ever to be heard
Or the beauty of art in whatever form
To weather the centuries
To evolve and grow
To what today we know
But take for granted
From the ancient drawings on cave walls
To the intriguing hieroglyphics of Ancient Egypt
To the words of Shakespeare
To the art and literature of modern-day form
The nonsensical, the whimsical, the tragical
The magical of both
The freedom to express
The joy of sharing of such magic
The loss of which would be tragic

## MOTHER'S DAY
## EILEEN FRANCIS BROWNE
## 27/03/1935 - 03/09/2004

It is again that time of year
I won't deny that I will shed a tear
Or two for you
For I miss you terribly still
And I always will
Many a time *when* alone
I really miss picking up the phone
To have a good old chat
About nothing more than this or that
Or a good old moan
I just want you to know
Mum, I love and miss you so
And I always will
So, until the day we meet again
With all my love I wish for you today
A very Happy Mother's Day

**MY DAD**
**ROBERT WILLIAM BROWNE**
**29/04/1932 - 06/11/1973**

When I think of you Dad
I often feel very sad
Not just for me
But my siblings too
For we had the best
Of dads in you
Your body constantly wracked in pain
Always a smile on your face
Never one to complain
Always a smile on your face
The love you had for mum
So clear to everyone
As was your love and pride
In each one of us children five
Then from us you had to leave
The angels came for you that awful day
Leaving everyone who knew you to grieve
Now reunited with our beloved Mum
Dad that day will one day come
When we will meet again
Until then I just want to say
Miss you, love you
Happy Heavenly Father's Day

## LESLIE MALCOLM
13/02/1958 - 31/08/1960

A little boy's face looks out from the frame
Leslie Malcolm is your name
Long life you never got to know
With the angels you had to go
Often have I wondered over time
Just how fine a young man you could have been
Like you younger brothers three
Behind your beautiful eyes
Hides the desperate pain
You were sadly born with cancer on the brain
A beautiful child of all accounts
Suffer did you so
Long before the days of chemo
You were my big brother
I never got to know
I sat snuggled in your arms
In the photo taken before you had to go
Treasured are the memories of you
Sweet little boy you were only two
Now reunited with your mummy and daddy who
loved you so
Leslie Malcolm
Forgotten you never will be

## MY OLD FRIEND

I smile every time I look at you
Together we have grown old
How many secrets have you been told
How many stories do you know
Would you dare to share
From the tearful tantrums of a toddler
To the angst of a hard done by teenager
From the kisses and cuddles
To the heartfelt putting the world to rights
You have always been there
Never to judge or to criticise
But to comfort and to give imagined advise
Once so new and pristine
Now the scruffiest ever to be seen
But Panda, my dearest old friend
I promise you this
You are mine to the very end

## THE FINAL COUNTDOWN

It is the final countdown
A door behind me is closing
As the one before me opens
I have given twenty-one years
Filled with much laughter and sadly some tears
Lifelong friendships made
Never to be broken
Now is the time for beginnings new
Because the time has now come
With work I have done
But don't think for one moment
Mr parky that you have won
I have so much I want to do
And as I stare out into future
I know there are many more
Life's adventures in store

## BUTTER ON MY TOAST

All I wanted was a bit of butter on my toast
But for me it is more of a challenge than most
Because of a "dodgy" brain
Even buttering toast is a bloomin pain
Opening the tub is in itself a feat
Dry toast I do not wish to eat
So why is something normally so simple
Being so difficult today
When I was able to do much more yesterday
No two days are the same
But I am fed up with this brain game
All I want is to be able to butter my toast
But thanks to Parkinson's
Today it just isn't to be
So, it's just a mug of black coffee for me
As the toast sails in the air like a Frisbee.

## CLICKETY CLACK

Watching the trees rush by
As the train rumbles on
Clickety clack, clickety clack
Speeding along the track
The soft roll of the carriage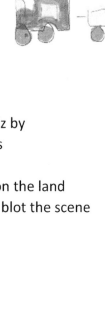
Gently rocks you to asleep
But not for long
Too much to see
Looking out of the window
You watch in awe as the fields whiz by
Looking like giant patchwork quilts
Of browns and greens
Spotting cows and sheep grazing on the land
Then passing many a scrapyard to blot the scene
Clickety clack Clickety clack
The train runs upon the track
Bringing you nearer to the station
Closer to your destination
At last you arrive
And now to survive
The hustle and bustle
As fellow passengers
Dragging their case
Join in the manic race

To get off the train
To catch their connection
To their destination
And it all starts again
With a clickety clack clickety clack
The next train speeds along the track

## SITTING IN THE VETS

Sitting in the vets with my cat
Listening to other pet mums and dads chat about
this and that
Some dogs growling
Others shaking
My cat is meowing and howling
Other pet owners nod their head
In greeting
Not a word is said
A giggle and an aah
Is uttered
As a dog walks by
With a huge cone on his head
The look of embarrassment and shame in his eye
Our turn arrives
Everything is ok
Apart from my bank balance
Now it is my turn to cry

## SOME DAYS

Some days the words they flow
Across the page
Feeding the imagination as they go
Telling a story for all to hear
Giving a smile or maybe even a tear
But there comes the day
When your words have nothing to say
You fear there may be no more
It is your mind telling you to rest
And to not fear
The words are waiting quietly
In the depths of your mind
For when you are ready
And allow you to find
Them once more

## WE DO GET THERE

Life is never a picnic
For some it can be tougher
Than for others
The unfairness of it all could bring us down
Keep us down
It is a continuous daily fight
Not to give in
Not to let the bugger's win
Simple tasks become proud achievements
Yes, it takes us longer
Than it ever did before
But we get there
Some of us shake rattle and roll
Some of us as stiff as a board
But we get there
Our dexterity getting slower
Some days we can write a novel
The next not even our name
No two days are ever the same
But we get there
Doing up button, pulling up zips
As for bra clips
Just don't you dare go there
But we get there
We do not need
Some jumped up bureaucrat
Decide whether we can do this
or whether we can do that
Because the cruelty of our disease

Is it slowly takes away our ability
Without someone else robbing us of our dignity
A little more respect
Would be kind
Look past the name and number
And you will find
Stubbornness and resolve
A desire to live a life as full as can be
Within our capabilities
Despite our disabilities
Because we really do get there
Eventually

## WHAT IS POETRY

What is poetry?
A play with words
Used over centuries of time
To tell a story?
Of loss or of glory
Of hopes and fears
Happiness and tears
Nonsensical or classical
Tragic or magical
Or just plain silly
What is poetry?
Good question!

## SO WHAT

Ok ... so what ...
So I have Parkinson's
Is that it ... is that my lot ...
No way
Even though its a fight every day
I am not ready to give in
I am not ready to let it win
Don't get me wrong
It is a battle not so easy
And some days
I don't always feel so strong
And the fight can wear me down
But not for too long
The positives are outweighing the negatives
The love of my family and friends get me through
And there is so much I still want  to do
And despite Parkinson's I still have a life to live

Printed in Great Britain
by Amazon

22609380R00069